The Seasons of Harold Hatcher

The Seasons of
Harold Hatcher

by Mike Hembree

Photographs
Mark Olencki

HUB
CITY
writers
project

2000

Friends of Hub City

Skyland Special
Phifer/Johnson Foundation
Spartanburg Herald-Journal

Peach Queen
Arkwright Foundation
The Arts Partnership of Greater Spartanburg
Jo Ann Bristow
Mr. and Mrs. Winston Hardegree
Agnes Harris
Dorothy and Julian Josey
Mrs. Roger Milliken
Olencki Graphics, Inc.
Price's Store for Men

Southern Crescent
Bea and Dennis Bruce
Colonial Trust Co.
Sara and Paul Lehner

Carolina Special

Dr. and Mrs. Mitchell H. Allen
Mr. and Mrs. Robert Allen
Mack and Kathy Neal Amick
Mr. and Mrs. W.D. Bain Jr.
First South Bank
Carolina Southern Bank Foundation
Valerie and Bill Barnet
Mr. and Mrs. Thomas Bartram
Dr. and Mrs. Charles Bebko
Shirley Blaes
Mr. and Mrs. Glen B. Boggs II
Dr. and Mrs. James Bradof
Pat Brock
Mellnee G. Buchheit
Sarah Butler
Mrs. W. Marshall Chapman
Mr. and Mrs. Arthur Cleveland
Mr. and Mrs. John Cleveland Cobb
Dr. and Mrs. Robert Cochran
Mr. and Mrs. Richard Conn

Mr. and Mrs. Paul Cote
John and Kristin Cribb
Nancy Rainey Crowley
Frances Davis
Mr. and Mrs. James Dunlap
Dr. and Mrs. William C. Elston
Mr. Duncan and the Rev. Beth Ely
Jean Erwin
Dr. and Mrs. Harold E. Fleming
Gordon and Karen Floyd
Dr. and Mrs. Sidney Fulmer
Mr. and Mrs. Billy Gossett
Margaret and Chip Green
Mr. and Mrs. Tom Grier
Benjamin and Tanya Hamm
Mr. and Mrs. Newton Hardie
Mr. and Mrs. Peyton Harvey
Mr. and Mrs. J. Thomas Hollis
Doug and Marilyn Hubbell
Bob and Lisa Isenhower

Sallie and Bill James
Mr. and Mrs. Stewart H. Johnson
Wallace Johnson
Mr. and Mrs. Charles W. Jones
Mr. and Mrs Charles D. Kay
Dr. and Mrs. Cecil F. Lanford
Mr. and Mrs. Paul Lehner
Mr. and Mrs. Fred M. Lockman Jr.
George Loudon
Alan and Mary Beth Lyles
Mr. and Mrs. Frank Lyles
Dr. and Mrs. Nathaniel Magruder
Thomas Matthews
Dan and Kit Maultsby
Byron and Linda McCane
Dr. and Mrs. Dean McKinney
Bob McMichael
Les and Betty McMillan
Mr. and Mrs. E. Lewis Miller
Karen and Bob Mitchell

Carolina Special (continued)

Nancy Moore
Mr. and Mrs. Douglas B. Nash
Nancy Ogle
Mr. and Mrs. Dwight Patterson
Mr. and Mrs. Edward P. Perrin
Mr. and Mrs. Robert V. Pinson
Sigmund Pickus and Janet Wilson
Gary and Anne Poliakoff
Dr. and Mrs. Jan Postma Jr.
Norman Powers
Mr. and Mrs. Norman Pulliam
Mr. and Mrs. Philip Racine

Mrs. Eileen Rampey
Mr. and Mrs. William B. Ramsey III
Karen Randall
Angela Rogers
Mrs. Gail D. Rodgers
Spartanburg Development Council
Mr. and Mrs. George Stone
Eric Tapio and Erin Bentrim-Tapio
Mr. and Mrs. Jess G. Taylor
Bill and Kristin Taylor
Betsy Wakefield Teter
Mr. and Mrs. Bob Tillotson

Charles and Sharon Tillotson
Elizabeth H. Wakefield
Mr. and Mrs. J. W. Wakefield
Mr. and Mrs. John T. Wakefield
Mr. and Mrs. David Weir
Mrs. Mary G. Willis
Jeffrey R. Willis
Dennis and Annemarie Wiseman
Brad Wyche
Cynthia and Stephen Wood
Kerry Scott Wood
Wm. Grantham Wood

Piedmont Limited

Anne Almers
Sue Almers
Diecy Gray Brennemann
Mrs. Thomas C. Breazeale
Mr. and Mrs. William Burns
Jesse Cleveland
Leah Kalis-Denda
Benjamin Dunlap
Nancy Dunn
Elaine Eilenberg
Dr. and Mrs. George Fields Jr.
Dr. Maxwell Goldberg
Gary and Carmella Henderson
Sally Hitchmough
Sam Howie
Clarence and Dee Johnson
Mr. and Mrs. John Karegeannes
Ernie Lambert

John Lane
Dr. and Mrs. Joseph H. Lesesne
Ann H. Lewis
Mike and Louise Lythgoe
Mr. and Mrs. Larry T. McGehee
E. Gibbes Patton
Curt McPhail
Mr. and Mrs. Mickey Pierce
Mrs. Roy S. Powell
Anita Stoddard
Elizabeth C. Taylor
Thomas V. Thoroughman
Gerald Thurmond
Joan Tobey
Mr. and Mrs. John Turpin
Mary Walter
Dave and Linda Whisnant
Suzanne and John Zoole

**Publication of The Seasons of Harold Hatcher
has been made possible by a substantial gift from the
Spartanburg County Foundation.**

ISBN 1-891885-09-X
First printing, January 2000

Hub City editor, Betsy Wakefield Teter
Cover and book design by Mark Olencki
Photography editors, John Lane, Christina Smith, and Karen Waldrep
Family support, Mom, Dad, Mildred, Diana, and Weston
Printed and bound by McNaughton & Gunn, Inc. in Saline, Michigan

Photo, "Snow on Heavenly Bamboo," by Linda McHamm

Hub City Writers Project
Post Office Box 8421
Spartanburg, South Carolina 29305
(864) 577-9349 • fax (864) 577-0188
www.hubcity.org

Table of Contents

Acknowledgements

The task of writing a book is often lonely but never solitary. People who regularly visit Hatcher Garden and Woodland Preserve and some who are unlikely ever to see its beauty contributed to these pages.

First, a big thank you to Alice Hatcher Henderson, who guided me through the often-tangled landscape of her father's long life, answering every question and providing valuable suggestions.

Dr. Robert Powell of Converse College offered knowledge and advice on the thousands of plant species in the garden, and Walter Soderberg, one of the first to endorse Harold Hatcher's dream, shared years of memories of work alongside his friend.

Thanks to Connie Melton for having the idea, Kelly Petoskey for helping to make it work, Mark Olencki for designing the book, and Betsy Teter and the board of the Hub City Writers Project for giving me the opportunity to tell the story.

The reference staffs of the Spartanburg County Library, the Greenville County Library and the South Carolina State Library were very helpful, as were Ruth Perkins and Evelyn Givens at the Green County (Kentucky) Public Library and Harold Worthley at the Congregational Library in Boston.

Thanks, also, to Dot Jackson and Jimmy Cornelison, fellow travelers in the endless pursuit of both the perfect sentence and the best mountain backroad. Debate continues on both fronts.

My wife, Polly, and children, Holly, Stacey and Chris, were sources of inspiration through another long project. Each has my love and admiration.

Finally, thanks to Teresa and Don Caine, gracious hosts and potential innkeepers, for use of a wonderful writing retreat in the Blue Ridge Mountains.

— *Mike Hembree*

Introduction

Hatcher Garden and Woodland Preserve is an eight-acre oasis in the southwestern corner of the city of Spartanburg, South Carolina.

It is a place apart, a forest in a town, a quiet, green swath dropped in among concrete and asphalt and the sounds and smells of the city.

Less than a hundred yards from the busy come-and-go of John B. White Boulevard, one of Spartanburg's most heavily traveled four-lanes, the garden is home to plants and animals more commonly found in the lush countryside. Its ponds, stream water, deep-green forest and winding trails paint a dramatic contrast to the world outside.

Yet more remarkable than this city sanctuary is the man who gave it life and has nurtured it for three decades.

Hatcher Garden and Woodland Preserve is the continuing, flourishing dream of Harold Hatcher, who grew up in poverty in Kentucky tobacco country and struggled against the odds to turn his life into one of promise and fulfillment. After spending a long career working in civil rights and social action causes, Hatcher moved to Spartanburg in 1969 and shortly thereafter began work in his backyard on what would become one of the Southeast's most impressive though understated public gardens.

Today, thousands visit its trails and quiet places, few knowing the story of the unique and complex man who brought it to life.

In the words of Converse College botany professor Robert Powell, Harold Hatcher "took a sow's ear and turned it into a silk purse" in the 30-year journey of transforming the Hatcher Garden into a natural showplace. In a much more personal way, he accomplished much the same sort of miracle within himself.

This, then, is the story of one man and his piece of the good earth.

Chapter 1
Spring

Spring comes to Hatcher Garden and Woodland Preserve on the wings of robins, in the riotous color of blooming redbud trees and in the delicate beauty of tiny wildflowers pushing through the earth.

The long, thin branches of winter jasmine arch toward the ground in ribbons of bright yellow. Cherry blossoms shout. Daylilies, a vibrant green, hold the promise of brilliant color to come.

Dogwoods, silent in winter, will be next on the color palette, bringing splashes of white to woods still asleep. Azaleas, the dogwoods' partners in upstate South Carolina's spring dance, will flower in tandem, their blooms a rainbow of colors on the banks of trails and under tall pines. White blossoms ignite a willow tree, and blooms cascade across the limbs of a star magnolia.

Swaying in the first warm winds of March are long limbs of poplar, oak, sweetgum, maple and hickory, waiting for the signal to push spring green into the air. Evergreens—hemlocks, English ivy, mountain laurel, rhododendron—boast of bold emerald color held over through winter. Hundreds of aucuba bushes, dark green with golden flecking, weave along with the trails, some showing reddish fruit left from December.

Leaves of copper decorate beech trees, spangling the early-spring forest.

Rows of daffodils blossom with fiery beauty, leading the showy march of color to come in flower beds spread across the garden. Green shoots of oak-leaf hydrangea thrust up.

In the understory, squirrels and chipmunks hustle about. Crows and mockingbirds chatter in the high trees. Toads spring into the ponds, barely noticed by the resident ducks. Somewhere, lost deep in the ivy, a northern water snake comes to life in the new spring and begins the search for food.

Winter's gone.

In this corner of the world, the spring of 30 years ago was quite different. Much of the land behind the residences along John B. White Boulevard was in a state of ill health. Eroded, overgrown, littered, in many ways forgotten.

Stepping into that silent spring was Harold Hatcher, who moved to Spartanburg from Indianapolis, Indiana, in April 1969. A self-taught student of gardening since the 1940s, Hatcher came south in large part because of weather conditions and seasonal changes that made gardening an attractive undertaking. His daughter, Alice, lived in Spartanburg, and he and his wife, Josephine, had become familiar with the area after making several visits.

Almost certain that he would retire in 1972, Hatcher knew upon his arrival in town that the focus of his retirement years would be gardening. In looking around Spartanburg for a place to live, he had a priority—a spot with natural water and big trees. He found two acres on the east side of town, near Alice's home, and bought the property for $9,000. The land had a stream and a waterfall, and Hatcher began dreaming about the house he and Josephine would build there and about the landscape they would create.

That eastside location, on Perrin Drive, might have become the Hatcher Garden but for property that appeared, almost by chance, on the other side of Spartanburg. Still pondering what approach to take on his new land, Hatcher bought a house with a small lot at 124

Briarwood Road, off John B. White Boulevard on the west side of town. The house was similar to one the family had owned in Indianapolis, and the backyard was pleasant, if small. There was a big elm tree, a tulip poplar and an oak.

The Briarwood house was to be a temporary residence while the Hatchers built a home on the east side, but that plan changed when Harold and Josephine more closely examined the woods that grew behind them on Briarwood—an apt name, as they discovered. From the rear of their backyard, they could see tall pines reaching to the sky and large hardwoods spreading over a stream. Vines, briars and other undergrowth covered the area beyond the backyard, but, nevertheless, it was inviting to the curious.

"My wife fell in love with the house right away because it was so much like our house in Indianapolis," Hatcher said. "I gradually got reconciled to it when I discovered the woods behind it. It had a lot of potential."

Potential—but little else. The land, once home to cotton fields, was badly eroded. Big gullies cut slashes across the property. The ravines had become dump sites for refrigerators, mattresses, tires and other refuse. It was not a pretty sight, but it sparkled in Hatcher's mind's eye. He could see what it might become.

"You almost needed a ladder to get across the first gully back there," he said. "I had to get a pruner to get through the vines. After the first big rain we had, we had a flood come across the backyard. I went back there to see where all the water was coming from. There was a little stream, but the rainwater had filled up the ravine and came rushing on down by the house. I wondered where so much water could come from. I walked back in the woods and could see how the flooding happened with the land being so eroded and the ravines collecting all the water that was running across it."

It was land that had been robbed of its nutrients by cotton farming and cleared of its topsoil by rushing rainwaters. To Hatcher, though, it was magic waiting to happen. Through the undergrowth, despite the harsh treatment visited upon the land, he could see the beginnings of his dream.

Although he didn't own the property behind the house, Hatcher investigated and concluded that it might be available in the future. The two-acre lot on the east side was suddenly expendable. Hatcher sold it for $14,000.

In Spartanburg, Hatcher had been hired as director of Piedmont Community Actions, a federally financed antipoverty agency. Josephine was a kindergarten teacher in Spartanburg School District Six. In the late afternoons and on weekends, they began the process of turning their small backyard —and, later, the woods to the rear of the property—into an attractive home for shrubs, flowers and young trees. In virtually every spare moment, they built flagstone walks and stone retaining walls and brought new life to the old neighborhood.

Soon after the move to Briarwood and the sale of the eastside property, Hatcher took the first step toward developing what eventually would become the Hatcher Garden and Woodland Preserve. He bought three acres behind the Hatcher house for $2,000 and, as he describes it, "got busy on it right away."

The early 1970s were busy years in the Hatchers' garden. There was much to do. Hatcher retired from PCA in 1972 at the age of 65 and devoted full time to gardening.

The first huge gully on the property was filled in the first months. Adding to the old appliances and other trash people had dumped on the site, Hatcher piled brush from the property into the ravine and covered it with dirt, giving him, for the first time, a clear walkway into the back of the property.

In reworking the land, Hatcher was assisting nature in a process scientists call old-field succession, a colorless term for the evolution of land from barren field to host for mature vegetation, or large-growth timber such as oaks and hickories. Typically, a Piedmont farm field that is abandoned or neglected for several years will begin to show clumps of crabgrass. Horseweed, aster and broom sedge will follow. Then pine trees will begin showing above the ground cover. The pines will rule the field for about 25 years, precursors to the hardwoods that eventually will crowd out virtually everything else. The evolution from farm field to deciduous forest will be complete—a process that takes several generations.

The property at the rear of 124 Briarwood Road was well into this process when the Hatchers arrived in 1969. Tall Virginia pines grew on the upper side of the land, and hardwood trees were beginning to take over the banks of the small stream. Harold Hatcher stepped into the process and accelerated it.

"This was an old, beat-up patch of worn-out cotton fields that had already started to heal," said Robert Powell, a Converse College botany professor familiar with the Hatcher Garden property. "Harold came in and enhanced it and made it a good garden. By him working with nature, this eventually will come back to a pristine forest."

Hatcher began his part of the recovery with new plants, the first of thousands that would be added to the property and its adjoining acres. The very first to be put in the soil, near the backyard of the Hatcher home, were rhododendrons, a showy late-spring shrub with exquisite flowers.

The rhododendron was a logical first choice for Hatcher. Sometimes difficult to grow but impressively beautiful at maturity, it is a regal addition to any garden.

"I had read about it a lot while living in Indianapolis," he said. "It was a favorite of successful people. And my ambitions led me to anything that resembled personal success and acclaim. The only place I had seen them in Indianapolis was in a successful lawyer's spacious yard. I stopped there one day and parked the car on the street and walked up to get a close look at them. He came out while I was looking and told me not to get too close, that they didn't like the soil being trampled near them."

Hatcher joined the American Rhododendron Society and attended a national convention of the group in Seattle. While on the trip, he bought about a hundred varieties of the shrub and brought them home to Spartanburg, where many found spots in the garden in a former pine thicket that had been attacked by pine beetles. The garden now is home to many splendid mature rhododendrons, and Hatcher recently planted a new batch.

The garden's first months gave Harold and Josephine many opportunities to work together, he clearing the pine fields of brush and undergrowth and planting the first shrubs, she planting azaleas (eventually more than a thousand), wildflowers and perennials and bringing the first color to the landscape. They saw the still-rough garden spot as a place of rest and beauty, an escape from everything else in the world, something worth protecting, nurturing, growing.

Others came and saw and agreed.

Walter Soderberg was the first. He and Hatcher met at a Spartanburg Men's Garden Club meeting in 1971, Soderberg having moved to Spartanburg from Hopedale, Massachusetts, in October 1970. Nearing retirement, Soderberg had time on his hands, and he wandered over to see Hatcher's project. Soon, he was stopping by almost every day, helping Hatcher clear brush, fill gullies and plant trees. He thus became the first in a long line of volunteer workers who have helped to speed the garden's evolution.

"I retired in 1978 from a part-time job, and from then on I was there a lot," said Soderberg, now 85. "Harold needed the help. There was a lot to do. He needed somebody else around. You never knew what he was going to try to do. I came in one time and he was way up on a 30-foot ladder with a chainsaw in one hand, leaning over trying to saw off a limb. He was fearless. I yelled at him, 'Harold, get down from there!'"

In addition to planting many trees that now fill much of the Hatcher Garden understory, Soderberg also helped Hatcher with another important project. In order to raise money to fund the work in the garden and the purchase of plants, Hatcher bought several older houses in the John B. White Boulevard area over a period of years, renovated them and put the rental money in a garden fund. He and Soderberg did most of the renovation of the houses.

"A lot of what we've done wouldn't have been possible without the rental income from those old houses," Hatcher said. "I'd buy a house that was in disrepair, fix it and rent it out, then duplicate the process."

The growth of the garden continued through the 1970s. Hatcher obtained additional adjacent property, enlarging the garden in an L shape from the Briarwood Road area to John B. White Boulevard, creating the entrance that now welcomes visitors.

Trails were established. Hatcher, Soderberg and other volunteers built a series of ponds to hold rainwater and storm runoff and an irrigation system so that the garden's plants and trees would have an unending water supply. More and more trees and plants were added. English ivy was transplanted from the Hatchers' daughter's property on the east side of town. Flower beds and a gazebo were built near the new front of the garden in an area that once had housed chicken coops. Hatcher made an agreement with the city of Spartanburg for city workers to dump dead leaves collected around town every autumn at the garden site, providing him with valuable mulch for the hungry soil.

Many new workers joined the list of garden volunteers. Men's Garden Club members, Spartanburg Garden Club Council members, neighborhood volunteers—all helped.

In the center of it all was Hatcher, who had educated himself about landscape design and horticulture. He went to sleep every night reading library books about propagating plants, testing soil, pruning trees, composting and the dozens of other tasks necessary in such an endeavor. He and Josephine did the work themselves or depended on volunteers for a simple reason—"There was no money to hire it done," he said. And also because it filled Hatcher with a joy he had never known. "I was glad to see the sun come up because I could get up and work," he said. "I didn't join organizations. I didn't do anything else. I just worked here. I couldn't wait to do the next thing."

There were many next things. More trails. A large observation deck (funded by the Men's Garden Club, as would be many garden projects over the years) overlooking the garden's stream. More flower beds. Construction of a 10-foot rock waterfall. The planting of shrubs and trees of many kinds and colors. Clearing. Weeding.

Gardening.

Hatcher's first significant attraction to gardening developed while the family lived in Indianapolis in the 1940s. He landscaped their property and was a leader in designing landscape projects at his church and office. He and

Josephine grew a vegetable garden, and he rented property so that employees of his company could grow their own vegetables. By 1950, landscaping had become his major hobby, and big trees had become his passion. They still stir him like little else. "He loses one of his best friends when a tree goes down," said Soderberg. "It hurts him to cut one up."

Late in the 1970s, the Hatchers' work in the woods behind Briarwood Road began to attract attention. Visitors to the Hatcher home would walk into the backyard, see the clearing in the woods beyond and investigate. Josephine's co-workers, first in School District Six and later at Spartanburg Methodist College, came for picnics and stayed longer, intrigued by the garden. Eventually (there was no formal "opening"), the garden went "public," and visitation steadily increased as word spread of its beauty.

Hatcher's work continued into the 1980s. In 1987, nearing 90 years of age, he decided to give the garden, by then a thriving woodland sanctuary, more permanent protection by donating the property to the Spartanburg County Foundation, then directed by James Barrett, a friend of the Hatchers. "I was wondering all the time about what would happen when I was gone," Hatcher said. "Would there be enough people to appreciate it, to keep it up, to not let it grow up in vines again?"

The proper documents were signed on November 25, 1987, extending the dream well into the years beyond his time. Other than the official transfer of ownership, however, little changed. Hatcher continued to work in the garden every day and to direct its progress.

There were more additions. A gardening shed, pavilion area, greenhouse and parking lot were built near the entrance. Hatcher, after hearing a handicapped woman say the trails were difficult to negotiate, paved several of them. The Spartanburg Technical College horticulture department got involved in design and planting, giving its students practical experience. More volunteers signed on. And, significantly, Hatcher got the assistance of what he calls public service workers, or people assigned to service jobs in the community as a way to "work off" sentences for driving under the influence and other violations.

The arrival of the public service workers—hundreds have toiled at the garden over the years—gave Hatcher a much bigger work force ("free manual labor," he called it), and some new headaches. Some of the workers were eager and cooperative; others were bitter and antagonistic. Since some couldn't drive, Hatcher became a taxi service. "Some of them were good and some were bad," said Walter Soderberg, who worked beside many of the public service people in the garden. "Harold made them toe the line. But he'd get in there and do twice as much as any of them."

Hatcher had started work on his garden at the relatively advanced age of 62. Three decades later, although slowed by various health problems, he still yearns for morning and the challenge of another day of his dream.

❧ ❧ ❧ ❧

Harold Hatcher's introduction to the concept of the good earth as plant producer came not in a grove of tall trees but in the hard soil of Kentucky tobacco country. He was born on March 7, 1907, near Greensburg, Kentucky, to the tobacco-farming family of Overton and Edna Mitchell Hatcher, who had married in 1904. The Hatchers lived about three miles from Greensburg in Green County in south central Kentucky, an area sustained by the growing of burley tobacco. Coal mines fed the people of eastern and western Kentucky, and the northern part of the state was bluegrass horse country, but tobacco was king in Green and surrounding counties.

Typically, all family members participated in the growing of tobacco. By the age of six, Harold, dressed in ragged pants and shirt, was in the tobacco patch, planting and weeding. It is not a time he remembers with particular fondness.

"You set out the plants in rows about three feet apart," he said. "They had to be wide enough for a horse or mule to get through. First, you stooped over and pushed a peg in the ground. You had the plants in a bag or bucket. You'd take one out, put it in the hole and push the dirt up around it. Then you moved on about two feet down the row and did it again. It was backbreaking work for anybody, but you could do it once you got about six."

Then came weeding with a hoe—and worming, removing destructive tobacco worms from the crop. "You had to pull the worms off by hand," he remembers. "You looked for them on the underside of the leaves. You could tell where there was a hole in the leaf or where it had been eaten on around the edges. Then you pulled him off and killed him. You usually pulled him so the innards squirted out.

"I remember one summertime when my girlfriend and sister were at the house. I wanted to show off in front of my girlfriend, so I showed them what a worm looked like—they were about two to three inches long and about a half-inch in diameter, and they squealed like girls are supposed to. Just to show I wasn't afraid of them, I put one in my mouth and bit off the head and spit it out."

They were impressed.

Worming lasted much of the summer, for it took a while for workers to move through the entire field. "Then when the plants got big enough, they had to be topped," Hatcher said. "You broke the top out and broke the sucker leaves growing off the sides so the big part of the plant would be good. A child eight to 10 could handle those kinds of things, as long as an adult followed up."

The harvest came in August. The most labor-intensive part of tobacco farming, this was a job for adults, for it involved cutting down the plants with a sharp blade. Then the stalks were stripped, a unique horticultural practice that happens in stages and involves a row of workers. The first person would pull off the "trash," or the part of the plant that couldn't be sold. The stalk would be passed on to the next person, and the leaves would be removed in "grades," depending on the quality.

In November, the tobacco was hauled into Greensburg to a warehouse, where it was sold to tobacco company representatives in an auction. The money earned in those warehouse auction sessions had to be stretched throughout the year by tobacco families. Burley tobacco, used primarily in cigarettes, continues to be a major cash crop in current-day Kentucky. The state leads the nation in its production.

Both of Hatcher's grandfathers were farmers, but his mother's father, John Archie Mitchell, refused to grow tobacco despite the fact that he had one of the biggest spreads—about 200 acres—in Green County, Hatcher said.

"He was well-known for his peculiarities," Hatcher said. "He played piano and organ, which was unusual at that time for that little rural community in the Kentucky hills, where education and culture were at a low level. He was a strong Presbyterian. He was regular in attendance at church and believed in Bible reading and prayer in the home. And he was stingy. That's one of the ways he put together a big farm without a mortgage. But he wouldn't have a stalk of tobacco on his place or let his children touch it. He grew livestock, sold calves and lambs and chickens and had a fruit orchard."

About a mile from the Mitchell farm was the smaller farm of William Hatcher, who grew tobacco and corn. The Hatchers were Baptists and Democrats. The Mitchells were Presbyterians and Republicans. They crossed paths when their children, Overton "Ote" Hatcher and Edna Mitchell, met and fell in love. Their marriage in 1904 started with practical presents—a horse and cow from John Archie Mitchell, who celebrated the weddings of all of his eight children in the same fashion.

The newlyweds lived with each set of parents for a while before saving enough money to buy a few acres of what Hatcher describes as "no-account land" located off a rural dirt road several miles from Greensburg. While Overton Hatcher was building the first of several small farm houses his family would call home, he rented a one-room log cabin from a nearby black farmer, an unusual practice in that time and a clear illustration of the struggle against poverty the family would face.

That cabin would be Harold Hatcher's first home. "When I discovered that a great American, Abraham Lincoln, not only came from the same state as me (Lincoln was born near Hodgenville, Kentucky) but also grew up in a log cabin, I figured the pattern was set for me," Hatcher said.

Despite making that connection, there was little reason to believe the young farm boy, the first child of poor parents, eventually would move on from tobacco country to other pursuits. Education was not a high priority in the Kentucky hill country in the early part of the century, and the birth of a son often was celebrated as the arrival of more help for the farm, another back to bear the burden.

Hatcher was fortunate, however. His grandmother, Betty Hatcher, and his aunt, Pinky Moss, taught him to read at a young age, filling his head with images that carried him far from Kentucky, to lands he could only imagine. Aunt Pinky gave him children's books every year at Christmas. "My aunt and her husband owned the only country store in that part of the county," Hatcher said. "She didn't have any children, and so she practically adopted me. I could always count on her reading a children's book to me. And my grandmother was in a wheelchair because of arthritis. She read a lot to me, too. I was fascinated by it."

The young Hatcher was more than ready when it came time to start school. That time didn't come until he was eight years old, and even then it was not a big event. Work on the farm took priority. School typically lasted only five months, Hatcher said, largely because work with the tobacco crop stretched through much of the year.

Hatcher didn't start school until his eighth birthday, in 1915, because his mother didn't want him walking a mile to the nearest school alone. He had to wait until his younger brother, Bruce, was old enough to accompany him.

They walked muddy dirt roads to Black Gnat School, a one-room log cabin in the community of Black Gnat. "There were five grades in that one room, and about 20 children, four or five in each grade," Hatcher said. "My grandmother and aunt had read to me, had given me a steady diet of it, and I breezed right through the first reader. I loved that. I could see that I could learn things and remember them. I liked school. I got a New Testament at the end of the year for perfect attendance, and then I had some more reading matter. There wasn't much else to read at home."

After the school at Black Gnat, Hatcher moved on to the nearby Blowing Spring school. He continued to perform well through the eighth grade, winning more New Testaments, staying near the top of his peer group, soaking up knowledge of new people and places. Intrigued by it all, he was becoming more and more interested in the world that could be found outside the narrow parameters of his existence.

"I used to dream that I'd own a big house on the top of the hill in Greensburg where I could look out over hundreds of acres and river bottoms below," Hatcher said. "I delivered newspapers to all those places. I wanted to be able to sit on a big front porch and see it all. I figured that would be the way to finish my life. But that dream gradually faded when I saw so many other things in the world."

Hatcher's next step in education would be to the county's only high school, located in Greensburg. It was a big move, one many of the area's children never made. If they advanced to the eighth grade, they typically left school to work full-time on the family farm, providing another pair of hands for the many tasks that always seemed to be waiting to be done.

This conflict between farm and school produced the first major crossroads in Hatcher's life and brought to the surface simmering difficulties within the Hatcher home. His father, wrestling with the land on a month-to-month basis, needed help and had assumed his oldest child— three other children would follow—would be available to him full time after the completion of eight grades of schooling. His mother saw the enthusiasm with which young Harold learned, and she yearned for her son to continue his education.

"Boys became too valuable on the farm to be going off to school and looking at a book," Hatcher said. "My dad had been waiting all this time for me to be able to help him in the tobacco crop year around, right through the summer. I found school so much fun, and I didn't want to give that up for a tobacco patch. My mother decided she'd back me on going to school. My father couldn't be convinced. There was a lot of fussing going on between them."

It wasn't their first disagreement. Nor their last.

Edna Hatcher worked a few hours a day as a clerk and postmaster at a country store near the Hatcher farm. Harold Hatcher remembers considerable conflict between his parents about the daily store visits of a one-armed mail carrier who arrived on horseback with a sack of letters. Overton Hatcher grew suspicious.

"My dad was very jealous," he said. "I was 12 years old and didn't see any cause for it at all. But I know they argued about it. Late one night everything in the house was quiet. I heard a noise downstairs. I knew it was my mother and father getting into a row. I rushed down the stairs. He had her backed up against the wall in the living room with his hands on her neck like he was choking her against the wall. I could see right away that it was more serious than I realized.

"One day when he and I were out hoeing tobacco, he decided to tell me about something that happened. He wanted to share it with somebody. I was the oldest child, and I guess there weren't too many others he could share it with. He suspected my mother was seeing the mail carrier outside the store. He said he saw my mother and the mail carrier go out the back of the store and down toward a barn owned by my uncle. He said he didn't think they were going down there for any bad purpose, but he didn't see any reason why they should be doing it.

"By that time, I had tears in my eyes. I couldn't see through them, and I started cutting down plants with the hoe. It was pretty strong medicine for a 12-year-old boy. I was a little sorry I had the only ears available to him."

The situation was made more difficult by the fact that his father often drank alcohol excessively, Hatcher said. Eventually, the couple would divorce, a rare occurrence in that time and place.

Edna Hatcher remained adamant that her son would attend school. She arranged for Harold to move into the town of Greensburg and live with her second cousin, who owned a drug store and lived on Main Street.

Living with Lapsley and Betty Wilson changed Hatcher's life. He attended Greensburg High School in a two-story building that also housed an elementary school. And he also got an education in the Wilson home. As a prominent business owner, Lapsley Wilson was on the board of the local bank, and his wife was on the school board. From his grandmother and aunt, Harold Hatcher had received an introduction to learning. In the Wilson home in Greensburg, the world opened to him.

"Their front room had a lot of bookcases filled with books," he said. "And they subscribed to magazines. I remember American Magazine in particular. It was filled with stories about how to succeed in life, the road to success from bottom to top. I swallowed all that hook, line and sinker."

Hatcher swept floors, washed dishes and did odd jobs to earn room and board with the Wilsons. He slept on a cot in the living room and walked to school every day. In the evenings, he talked to the three "old maids" who rented rooms upstairs.

After Overton and Edna Hatcher divorced, she moved into Greensburg with Harold's two sisters, Elizabeth and Julia, renting a room at a Presbyterian parsonage. Bruce stayed on the farm with his father but eventually joined the rest of the family. His parents remained friends after the divorce, Hatcher said, and his father gave his mother a diamond ring years after their separation, a gift that still puzzles him.

Hatcher graduated from Greensburg High School along with 15 classmates May 21, 1924. Honored as salutatorian, he gave a short speech, one he had practiced while tending cattle in the river bottom.

At 6 o'clock the next morning, Hatcher was at the railroad depot in Greensburg, ready to catch the Louisville & Nashville Railroad train to Louisville, 100 miles away. Convinced by magazine advertisements and discussions with friends that he could work his way through college, he intended to work in Louisville during the summer to save enough money to begin his freshman year at Indiana University in Bloomington in the fall. He boarded the train with a few clothes in an old suitcase and some money—less than $100, he estimates—he had earned painting houses in Greensburg.

Hatcher arrived in Louisville, rented a room in a rooming house downtown for $4 a week and got a job in the first place he stopped—the office of the Louisville & Nashville Railroad. To get there, he rode an elevator for the first time. The pay, for a clerk job stamping tickets for stations along the L & N line, was $50 a month. He also worked part-time in a candy store in the city, saving every dollar he could for the big step he would take in the very near future.

Harold and Josephine Hatcher on their wedding day

Chapter 2

Summer

By midsummer, a dark green canopy of leaves has spread over much of the Hatcher Garden, its tall oaks, maples, poplars and sweetgums providing a cloak of shade for the understory and forest floor below. The July visitor, having stepped off the sidewalk on John B. White Boulevard and out of the morning sun, might find the temperature 10 degrees cooler deep in the garden.

Daylilies greet the morning with splashes of vibrant color, decorating the banks of the ponds. Crape myrtles light the hillsides with pink and white fire. Butterfly bushes offer yellow and purple blooms to winged guests, who come by the hundreds, drawn to the flowers and the wide, open areas near the garden's entrance.

Hummingbirds fuss over trumpet flowers. Chipmunks scurry through the underbrush. Daisies, impatiens and petunias shine.

Cattails and Japanese honeysuckle ring the upper ponds, and flowering water lilies cross their surfaces. Small sugarberry trees grow on the banks. Dragonflies whir overhead. On the water, mosquito fern stretches out from the banks.

In the Healing Garden, a project of the Garden Club Council, parsley, golden sage, golden marjoram, chives and thyme greet the summer sun.

Along the trails, the gold tint on aucuba leaves marks the way. Lush ferns glow green on patches of earth underneath the tall trees.

The observation deck, the garden's centerpiece, offers a prime place to view the bursting glory of rhododendrons on the creekside. Dog-hobble, a water lover, its stems thick and leathery, spreads along the banks.

Benches provide pleasant spots to stop and listen to water tumbling over rocks and gurgling down the creekbed. The garden's lone natural spring feeds the lower parts of the property, sending water on to Fairforest Creek and, eventually, the Atlantic Ocean.

On almost any summer morning, Harold Hatcher can be found cruising the garden paths in battered old golf cart No. 38, a refugee from the fairways, a weary machine seemingly held together by duct tape and persistence.

❦ ❦ ❦ ❦

The girl's name is lost to Harold Hatcher's memory now, but the moment is crystalline in its profundity in his life.

At the end of his first year at Indiana University, Hatcher, having been involved in Presbyterian Church activities on campus, became a member of an interracial committee formed in the area. Made up of six whites and six blacks, the committee met for the first time at the home of a university sociology professor. "We were asked to introduce ourselves, tell where we came from, that sort of thing," Hatcher said. "I don't remember much about it except that when we got all the way around the room one of the three black girls said she was from my little hometown of 800 people, and I didn't even recognize her name. I found out later she was the daughter of a barber in town and that she grew up near me, and I had never seen her, never knew anything about her. And she was right there, just down the road from me."

Hatcher cries telling the story, a sense of astonishment about the circumstances still in his voice.

Hatcher grew up in a stringently segregated society in which the line between white and black was clearly drawn—and infrequently crossed. From an early age, he was taught that blacks were inferior to whites.

"Even though we grew tobacco, my mother kept us away from (smoking) it," Hatcher said. "She wanted me to be aware of the health hazard. She used her strongest ammunition. She told me if I drank coffee or smoked cigarettes I would turn black, 'like a nigger,' as she put it. And I believed it, even though I hadn't seen any people who had turned black."

A young black man named Clarence worked in the tobacco fields for the Hatchers. Although he and Harold, then about 10 years old, hoed weeds side by side and became friends, when lunchtime came, Harold's mother put her son's food on the dining room table and fed Clarence in the kitchen. "He was very personable and a favorite of mine," Hatcher said. "But my mother wouldn't let us eat lunch in the same room. She said it was custom that black and white people don't sit at the same table. I didn't see any sense to it."

At about the same time, an incident involving blacks and whites jarred Hatcher's thinking. Told all his life that blacks were inferior in all things, he found reason to think that he possibly wasn't being told the whole truth.

"The black school was near the corner of our farm, and we usually had to pass black kids walking to school," he said. "One day, a rock-throwing fight broke out between the two groups. We thought we were at a safe distance from the black kids, but I was suddenly struck in the head by a stone thrown by one of them. It hit me solid, and I remember thinking that nobody could have thrown it that far and with that accuracy. I was quite puzzled at this because I had heard so much from my parents and others about the inferiority of the black child. The fact was that neither I nor any of my friends could have thrown a rock so far and so accurately. This raised a question mark in my mind."

Ingrained for so many years, Hatcher's racial attitudes would begin changing only when he arrived at Indiana University, and even then the change would be gradual.

Hatcher first stepped onto the IU campus in Bloomington in mid-September 1924. It was the first time he had been outside Kentucky. "I was just staggered by the size of the campus, by the big buildings," he said. "It was just a new world for me. I really felt that if this wasn't heaven, it was the next thing to it. My life was starting over. I lived on that cloud until the first bump came along."

It arrived on the first day of classes. Driven to succeed and determined to do everything possible to impress his professors, Hatcher walked into his English composition class and headed for the front row. "At church they judged you on how close you got to the front row, so I thought being there would help," he said. "The seat next to me was open. A black student came in the door and sat down. It touched a button somewhere in me. Instinct took over. I had never even *heard* of integrated schools. I found myself walking to the back of the room to get another seat. There weren't any, so I stood.

"After class, I went to the head of the department and told him I wanted to transfer to another class. He told me he was from Kentucky, too, and understood my situation. He moved me to a class that didn't have any blacks."

Over the course of three years at IU (he finished

bachelor's degree requirements in that period), Hatcher saw his outlook on race relations and many other things change dramatically.

He arrived on the campus with burning ambition. The struggles he had seen in rural Kentucky made him determined to succeed in business, to make a name for himself, to make money.

And—he had decided—to be different. That thought became a nearly lifelong theme. In the early weeks at IU, with plans to get a degree in business administration and make it big in the business world, he could not have imagined how different "different" would become.

"Even while I was in high school, I was trying to develop a philosophy of life," Hatcher said. "I observed people. I came to the conclusion that most of them had some habit that they shouldn't have or weren't on the right road to ever amount to anything in life. The magazines in my cousin's home stressed working, saving, studying, developing your mind. That made sense to me. I had fun in school, and I could see it was fun developing your mind. It got you compliments. It built up your ego. So I boiled it down to a simple philosophy—be different."

Religion would have a significant impact on the course of Hatcher's life. Raised in the Presbyterian faith of his grandfather, he became a member of the Ebenezer Presbyterian Church near Greensburg at the age of 11. As a youth, he remembers categorizing churchgoers. "Baptists shouted, Methodists were somewhat more reserved, and Presbyterians were not at all emotional," he said. "I remember my Aunt Pinky taking me to the Baptist church. She would climb on the pew and holler.

"There was a revival meeting at the Presbyterian church, and the preacher asked, 'Which ones of you want to go to heaven? Raise your hands.' Heaven or hell—the choice seemed pretty clear to me. I had to raise my hand. Then he said, 'All of you who raised your hand come down front and kneel down and be challenged to lead a new life.' My Presbyterianism held on through college."

While at IU, Hatcher was concerned with much more than his studies. With little money saved and no financial support from home, he had to earn enough to live on and pay school costs. Arriving in Bloomington, 190 miles from Greensburg, that September, he rented a room in a house on the edge of the campus and got a job waiting tables at the sorority house across the street.

The girls, it turned out, were not impressed.

"After I worked there a few weeks, they told me they were going to have to let me go," Hatcher said. "The girls were objecting because I didn't change my shirt often enough. I wore a clean white jacket, but I guess it's very noticeable when you set a plate in front of someone and you have a dirty cuff underneath. I guess it was the old Kentucky hills showing in me. I hadn't found a way to get the money to pay for regular laundry service."

Undaunted, Hatcher walked downtown and, within the hour, had sweeping jobs at two Bloomington businesses. Later, he was recommended for a houseboy's job at the IU president's home. During his second Christmas in Bloomington, he chose to stay in town for the holidays, earning money by fueling coal-fired furnaces for residents who were visiting elsewhere.

He also worked hard in school. His IU transcript shows several C's in his freshman year, but by his final year the grade line held only A's and B's.

Hatcher was so impressed with Bloomington and the university atmosphere that he located a rental house near the campus and persuaded his mother to move there. She worked in the university cafeteria and later ran a boarding house for college students. Hatcher's brothers and sisters also moved to Bloomington, and each one attended college, traveling the path their brother had blazed. His father eventually arrived in town, too, working as a carpenter.

Hatcher was graduated June 6, 1927, with a degree in sociology, a dramatic departure from his original plans to concentrate on business courses. His experiences at IU, meshed with his background of poverty (and the fact that he didn't like accounting and business study), had convinced him that he should work toward solving the problems of poor people and helping them step up in life.

One way to pursue such a goal, Hatcher reasoned, was the ministry. He jumped at a partial scholarship offer to attend Chicago Theological Seminary, which was closely associated with the University of Chicago, located directly across the street.

Still longing for that place at the head of the class, Hatcher visited the seminary library soon after arriving on campus. Examining the shelf that held all the master's degree theses, he found the longest one and devoted himself to writing his at least one page longer.

And he did.

Hatcher wrote a complex study of the dozens of religions being practiced within the Loop, the transportation system that ringed Chicago's downtown area. From Baptist to Jewish to Spiritualist to Hindu, he attended a service in each place of worship, examined the neighborhoods from which their constituents came and reached conclusions about the impact of each.

From 1928 to 1930, Hatcher earned a master's degree in biblical literature and a bachelor of divinity. He also met the two people who would mean the most in his future—Josephine Timmerman, who would become his wife, and professor Arthur Holt, whose influence would direct much of the rest of his life.

Josephine Timmerman, a native of Palatine, Illinois, was studying religious education at the seminary. She also worked among the urban poor in Chicago. She and Harold had shared goals and values. By February 1930, a few months from graduation, they were engaged. "I was about to leave after proposing to her and having her accept," Hatcher remembers. "I was ready to say good night and go home. She said, 'Wait a minute. Don't I get a kiss?' That was my first one. Boy, I saw then what I had been missing."

They were married Aug. 19, 1930, in the seminary chapel in a ceremony marked by the participation of individuals from a variety of races and ethnic groups, including a Jewish rabbi and a Japanese student. Their vows were written in verse by the bride.

Holt, a professor of social ethics, had a major impact on both Harold and Josephine. Talking about his effect later, each said they saw him as important in their understanding of Christianity as a religion that emphasizes helping others, a concept known then as the "social gospel" and "applied Christianity" and a movement that worked toward erasing the historical barriers of race, religion, nationality and gender. The seminary and its church — then the Congregational Church, now the United Church of Christ—advocated that aspect of religious teachings with particular zeal in the late 1920s and early 1930s, a time of economic upheaval.

After his second year at the seminary, Hatcher accepted a position as a summer pastor at a small church in Billings, Montana. He said he enjoyed the freedom he experienced there but quickly concluded that the life of a full-time preacher was not his cup of tea, although he later would be ordained as a minister by the Congregational Church in a service at Broadway Tabernacle in New York City.

In his final year at the seminary, Hatcher requested a black student as a roommate. Arthur Gray, a student from Talladega, Alabama, roomed with him. "It helped rid me of more of my vestiges of race prejudice," Hatcher said. Gray would go on to become a prominent pastor in the Congregational Church—and the best man at Hatcher's wedding.

After seminary, Hatcher was awarded a fellowship for a year of study of religion and philosophy at the University of Marburg in Germany. He and Josephine spent their first year of marriage in Germany, arriving in Hamburg by boat to be greeted by surging Nazism and repeated talk of the name of Adolf Hitler. The Germans Hatcher encountered during his studies and in the countryside were quite different, though, from the images he had carried from childhood. Growing up during World War I, Hatcher had heard members of his family talk about their hatred for Germany and Germans, an emotion spurred, in part, by the death of a beloved family member, Arthur Mitchell (Hatcher's uncle), who was killed on a battlefield in France in the final weeks of the war.

"I was impressed by the German people," Hatcher said. "It was another prejudice I had to work through. My family had been prejudiced against anybody that was different—Northerners, Catholics, people with different accents, anybody different from their close associates."

The trip also undergirded an idea that Hatcher had been pondering, perhaps not altogether knowingly, for years—that of pacifism.

"I could remember having mixed feelings about shooting birds with a rifle I had gotten for a Christmas present as a kid," he said. "And I would back away from fights in high school. The part I liked least about going to Indiana University was its requirement that every male student take two years of military training. I helped form a group that publicly campaigned to make it optional. I was attaching a lot of importance to nonviolence in all forms. I didn't have any interest in fighting or violence of any kind and had decided that I wouldn't fight in a war."

After a year of study that included several side trips to other European countries, the Hatchers returned to the United States in the summer of 1931 and rented a small apartment near the seminary in Chicago.

Harold Hatcher, now holder of three degrees and a very different person from the big-eyed Kentucky freshman who had stepped in wonder onto the Indiana University campus seven years earlier, was ready for the world. And, maybe, ready to change it.

Harold Hatcher in the lower garden

Key volunteer Jess Taylor

Henry Pittman and Bob Almond transplanting young specimens

Kelly Petoskey, executive director

Harold Hatcher preparing a new rhododendron bank

Harold Hatcher, creator and founder of the Woodland Preserve

Variety of daffodils (*Narcissus* sp.) donated by Jack del Vroomen

Picnic area overlooking "the high waterfall"

Bullfrog on a lilypad (*Nymphoea* sp.) in a sunny pond below the gazebo

Tall bearded iris (*Iris germanica*, cultivar: "Clarence") and pollinator

View into the garden from the Hatchers' original property

Summer Science Camp with John Green walks past the upper pond

Lacecap Hydrangea (*Hydrangea* sp.)

Pond-side Plantain Lily (*Hosta* sp.) and hemlocks (*Tsuga canadensis*)

Fall scene near the gazebo

Sweetgum leaves and fruit (*Liquidambar styraciflua*)

Silhouette of compound leaves

Tulip Poplar (*Liriodendron tulipifera*) with turning leaves

Sun shining through ice covered hardwoods

Ice twig with leaf buds

Snow on Heavenly Bamboo (*Nandina domestica*)

Daffodil foliage and fallen leaves

Chapter 3

Autumn

Few spectacles in nature match that of an Eastern deciduous forest making the change from summer to fall, an annual delight that draws millions of tourists to colorful mountain ranges and highland areas from Georgia to Maine. Every autumn, the Hatcher Garden plays its part in this grand show.

The first hint of the color change comes from sourwood and blackgum trees, their leaves turning almost overnight to a deep reddish purple. They provide the signal for outrageous color to come, of vibrant reds and brilliant yellows and beautiful oranges, all spread from treetop to treetop in a patchwork quilt of seasonal finery. Maple, birch, oak, hickory, poplar, dogwood—all change, typically at different stages, so that the color wheel turns throughout the season.

Deep in the Hatcher Garden, this color change occurs against a burnished background of evergreen—smooth leaves of rhododendron and mountain laurel, elegant hemlocks, prickly hollies. The contrast of gold and green is striking.

Along the trails, crisp autumn air welcomes visitors. Falling leaves dance in their drop to the ground, bringing an autumn carpet to the forest floor. In the underbrush, squirrels dance about, beginning their forage work for the winter ahead.

And, it is harvest time.

In the upper reaches of the garden, on certain days in October and November, Harold Hatcher pauses from the planting, weeding and clearing to collect the garden's edible bounty—pecans. The autumn of 1998 brought four bushels, providing snacks for Hatcher and friends for weeks to come.

One of the garden's pecan trees holds a special place in Hatcher's heart. Located on the western fringe of the garden, it is massive, perhaps 80 feet high, its huge limbs branching out 40 feet. Maybe a hundred years old, it probably was planted in what then was an open field and thus was given a lot of room to grow up and out, with little competition for sun and moisture.

In autumn, its size—and its fruit—are among the garden's major attractions, especially to a score of squirrels in the early morning hours.

❦ ❦ ❦ ❦

In 1931, Harold and Josephine Hatcher returned to the United States from a year abroad to find the country in the deepest valley of the Great Depression. Factories, banks and stores were closing, millions were jobless, bread lines were long.

Rejoining the Chicago seminary community, Hatcher accepted a job as a research assistant to Arthur Holt, the professor who had led him into concentrated study of social ethics. He made $100 a month and worked for Holt for about a year, researching, among other things, farming problems. Farm prices dropped dramatically during the depression, forcing many farmers to abandon land their families had owned and worked for generations. Mortgage and tax problems resulted in the forced sale of more than

10 percent of United States farms in the early 1930s. Some farmers burned corn, their cash crop, for fuel because they couldn't afford oil.

Hatcher's work in the farm arena led to a full-time job. In 1932, he accepted a position as secretary-treasurer (in effect, director) of the Illinois division of the Farmers Educational and Cooperative Union of America. Also known as the National Farmers Union, the organization represented the liberal wing of the farm movement, attempting to link small-farm owners into a force that would give them a bigger voice in reforms. The NFU typically supported policies that would enhance cooperative economic initiatives among farmers but opposed the concentration of capital in huge monopolies.

The situation was almost perfect for Hatcher, who saw a kindred spirit in the struggling farmer, a little person trying to rise above conditions, a gnat battling the giant. This was the raw frontier of social action, a first real-life classroom for a young man determined to make a difference.

He worked first from an office in Kankakee, Illinois, and later in Bloomington, Illinois. (The National Farmers Union Illinois office today is located in Springfield. The modern union has 300,000 member farm families nationally. The 1930s union probably was "a bit more militant" than the current organization, a spokesman said.)

Hatcher performed numerous tasks. He was writer, editor and distributor of the *Illinois Union Farmer*, the organization's monthly (later, more frequent) newspaper. He was a recruiter, traveling Illinois backroads in a 1927 Chevrolet, speaking at meeting after meeting, trying to convince farmers that unity—in particular the Farmers Union brand—was the answer to many of their problems. In one month in 1933, he drove 2,100 miles. "I was kicking up a ruckus for a 25-year-old," Hatcher said.

Part of the union's goal, as outlined in the newspaper, was "to secure for agriculture cost of production plus a reasonable profit" and "to unite the forces of organized labor, organized consumers, and organized agriculture." In an editorial in the March 21, 1934, *Illinois Union Farmer*, Hatcher wrote: "How can agriculture get equality? Will the New Deal do it? No, nor will a Raw Deal or a Square Deal. It will come only after agriculture has put itself in a position to demand and to enforce equality. That comes only through organization and collective effort."

The pay wasn't impressive—$125 a month, and Hatcher's traveling expenses came from that total. He and Josephine, who helped him in the office, benefited from gifts of food from farmers.

The work was dangerous. Rival farm groups interrupted meetings of farmers who had gathered to hear Hatcher's spiel. "Some guys came into one meeting to, they said, run me out of town," he said. "They said they were going to give me a good tar-and-feathering for the things I had printed or said that were damaging to their efforts. They got hold of me in a meeting, dragged me down the stairs and put me in the car headed home. At another meeting, a guy grabbed me by the collar as I was speaking and twisted it, choking me. The meeting terminated about that time."

The pressures of the farmers union job also contributed, Hatcher said, to a great tragedy in the young couple's early life together. Working long hours and traveling many miles, Hatcher needed Josephine's support to keep the office functioning. She was six months pregnant on a July day in 1933 when the strain of the situation cost them dearly.

"She was helping me get the newspaper to the post

office on time," Hatcher remembers. "It was almost a desperate effort to get it out. We were carrying it there, and that night she went into labor early. The babies— identical twin girls—were born about three months early. They didn't live a full day, partly because of the limited medical facilities of those days. That experience cut deep." The girls were named Laura and Celia.

During his three-year stay with the farmers union, buoyed by the fire of front-line activism and his fierce support for what he saw as the dispossessed, Hatcher "permitted my name to appear on the ballot," as he described it, in 1934 as a candidate for the United States Congress on the Socialist Party ticket. He and Josephine were both supporters of Socialist Party presidential candidate Norman Thomas, who ran in 1928, '32, '36, '40, '44 and '48.

It was a token effort, with Hatcher doing no substantive campaigning (in part because Josephine didn't want her conservative Republican parents to know about the decision). In the Nov. 6 election for two at-large Congressional seats from Illinois, Hatcher finished seventh among 12 candidates, receiving 13,580 (0.51 percent) votes. Democrats Michael Igoe and Martin Brennan were elected with more than 1,400,000 votes each.

Hatcher never ran for elective office again.

Arthur Holt re-entered Hatcher's life in 1935, opening the door for his next job change. Active in national affairs in the Congregational Church, Holt was a key player in the formation of the church's Council for Social Action, a new department established at the church's General Council meeting in Oberlin, Ohio, in June 1934. The Council for Social Action, conceived as a department that would be on a par with the church's missionary efforts, was created to address a wide array of social problems, including war, poverty, discrimination and labor troubles. It would act as the church's "Christian social conscience." Holt signed a document supporting the establishment of the council. It read, in part, that the church "will find itself as it loses itself in the struggle to achieve a warless, just and brotherly world . . ."

At Holt's urging, Hatcher was hired as the council's research director. His pay doubled immediately—to $250 a month. The Hatchers, now with an infant daughter, Alice, moved to New York City, where the Congregational Church headquarters was located.

The minutes of the church's General Council meeting in June 1936 at South Hadley, Massachusetts, list Hatcher as a member of the CSA staff and list his tasks, among others, as a "study of the oil scandals revolving around the name of Samuel Insull, . . . a study of the textile industry, and . . . other related subjects."

The CSA report included in the 1936 minutes lists four "chief fields of social concern for the church." They were international relations (specifically the threat of war), industrial relations (including unionism, civil liberties, standards of living), country life (farming economics) and race relations.

Much of Hatcher's work with the CSA involved writing for and editing *Social Action*, the council's twice-monthly educational publication. He researched and wrote about such topics as horse-track gambling, the automobile industry, textile mills and steel workers. Some of the research took him across the country, and the April 15, 1936, edition of *Social Action*, "The Textile Primer," included information he gathered on a trip to textile mills in and around Spartanburg. At the conclusion of a lengthy report, Hatcher recommends the establishment of minimum wages and maximum hours for textile workers, the abolition of child labor and an end to what he called discrimination against textile unions. He also suggested that the federal government buy or lease textile equipment and hire the unemployed to produce clothing for the poor.

Hatcher's work at the CSA also gained him a bit of national media attention. Attending an annual meeting of the General Motors Corporation while doing research for an article on auto workers' union activities, he stood during nominations for officers and recommended the election of a union official to GM's board of directors. "I was just suddenly struck with a deep urge to grasp the opportunity," he said. "I noticed everyone was turning and looking at each other in surprise and disbelief." His recommendation was not accepted, but descriptions of the incident appeared in several major news publications.

While working for the CSA, Hatcher also set up a grocery cooperative in his 13-story apartment complex on the lower east side of New York City, near Chinatown. He remembers delivering milk, which the co-op purchased from a dairy farmers' cooperative, along the halls of the 1,300-unit complex in the early morning hours.

"Everybody was looking for ways out of the depression," Hatcher said. "What we set up was a customer-owned business that was democratically controlled and run on a non-profit basis. We bought the milk wholesale and paid dividends to the co-op members in the form of shares. There were a lot of young married couples like us in the complex, and that type of co-op was attractive then."

His experience led Hatcher to his next job change. In 1938, he left the church office to become marketing manager for Eastern Cooperative Services, a consumer-owned wholesale grocery chain based in New York. Attending a national cooperative convention, he met a man associated with a retail co-op in Indianapolis. Discussions with co-op officials led to an offer of a job as manager of Cooperative Services in Indianapolis. Eager to move his family, which now included a son, Haskins, from metropolitan New York, Hatcher accepted the job, going to work in Indianapolis in 1940. He would stay with the group through 1958.

After the Hatchers arrived in Indianapolis, a second son, Thomas, was born on October 30, 1941.

The family had a Christmas party at home on December 20, 1943. That night, Thomas awakened his parents with a coughing spell. "We rushed him to the hospital, but he was turning purple by the time we got there," Hatcher said. Thomas died the next day of meningitis.

Two additional sons joined the family during the Hatchers' stay in Indianapolis. Allen was born October 23, 1944, and Andrew May 30, 1948.

Haskins, the couple's first son, died at the age of 22 in 1959. Living in Bloomington, Indiana, and enrolled in Indiana University's graduate school of music, he decided to visit his fiance in St. Louis. Instead of driving his decrepit early-model Ford, he chose to try to hop a freight train, "something he'd done before without incident," his father said. The train apparently was traveling too fast, however, and Haskins fell to the ground, fatally injured.

"I was awakened late that night by Allen telling me there had been a phone call that Haskins was dead," Hatcher said. "I had to go to the morgue to identify him. It was a sad day. He was a very adventurous sort. We camped a lot together, canoed, traveled to Colorado, climbed mountains. He was always ready to go, to do the next thing."

On a table in Haskins' apartment, the family found a Bible opened to Luke 9:62: "But Jesus said to him, 'No one, having put his hand to the plow, and looking back, is fit for the kingdom of God.'"

Rather than dwell on tragic losses, Hatcher said he is thankful for the successes of his three surviving children: Alice, a college professor in Spartanburg; Allen, a professor at Cornell University in Ithaca, New York; and Andrew, a computer systems analyst in Boston, Massachusetts.

Hatcher's major task in Indianapolis was managing a coal and heating oil delivery cooperative. The co-op's status improved quickly, and Hatcher moved the operation from an Indianapolis back street to the more vibrant central part of the city.

Hatcher also worked within the organization to hire minorities and empower them with positions of authority, a successful effort that attracted the attention of the American Friends Service Committee of the Quakers. In 1958, Hatcher became the executive director of Merit Employment, a Quaker-funded Indianapolis community service agency that sought to help blacks and other minorities overcome job discrimination.

"It was one of the most satisfying jobs I ever had," Hatcher said. "I tried to help blacks get jobs in large companies that previously had not employed minorities in certain job classifications. It took research. I went to schools around the city and sought out the best candidates and got them in the right positions. In a lot of cases, they were the first blacks to work at certain levels, like a bank teller or a clerk in a department store. The first reports were favorable, and other businesses started calling us to send them people."

While in Indianapolis, Hatcher crossed paths with a man destined to make history of a sensational sort in the late 1970s. The Rev. Jim Jones, charismatic and energetic, pastored one of the biggest churches in downtown Indianapolis. A white man, he reached out to blacks, and many joined his church. "I was working for better race relations in the broad sense, and he was, too," Hatcher said. "He was friendly with me. He was very evangelical, old-fashioned in his preaching. His personality was emotional. He was very different in personality and in theology from me."

In 1978, Jones, who had relocated to California and later to a jungle compound in Guyana, ordered 912 of his followers to drink cyanide-poisoned liquid in a mass suicide. Jones was found among them, a bullet in his head.

In 1961, Hatcher's work in Indianapolis attracted the attention of Indiana Governor Matthew Welsh, who was organizing the state's first Civil Rights Commission. In July, Welsh offered the commission's first directorship to Hatcher, and he accepted, reaching the pinnacle of his career.

Hatcher's staff investigated charges of discrimination filed by minorities in employment, public accommodations and housing. The commission moved against the current, fighting opposition from politicians, news media and much of the public. "I got more than a few threatening phone calls, calling me 'nigger lover' and things like that," Hatcher said. "It was a lot of pressure. We spent family time camping on Lake Michigan, getting away from it."

In 1963, the *Indianapolis Recorder*, a black weekly newspaper, named Hatcher to its Human Relations Honor Roll, saying his work "has brought the light of a new era in race relations throughout the length and breadth of Hoosierland."

Hatcher led the commission into the spring of 1969. By that time, the urge to move south was beckoning— and from several directions.

The commission job was less attractive than it had been, in part, Hatcher said, because of the arrival in Indianapolis of a Republican governor. Hatcher had been appointed by a Democrat. The Hatchers liked the Carolinas, having been to Spartanburg several times to visit Alice. They started looking for a home in the South.

"I was thinking of a place where I could garden all year," Hatcher said. "I wanted a place where I could have the right selection of plants—evergreens, blooming plants. At first, we thought of Asheville, but we found that the temperatures weren't that different from Indianapolis. And we had had enough snow. We gradually came to feel that Spartanburg was the right place for us."

Alice, who had moved to Spartanburg in 1962, suggested her father pursue a job at Piedmont Community Actions, a federally funded anti-poverty program that was seeking a director for its Spartanburg County office. Hatcher applied, got the job and moved to Spartanburg in April 1969.

In recommending Hatcher for the job in a letter to Mary Frances Oliver, acting director of PCA, former Indiana governor Welsh said Hatcher "is rather quiet but has great determination and persistence, coupled with tolerance and understanding, thus he was able to work very well with the white leadership all over Indiana, and at the same time achieve very great progress. The fact that Indiana has not had civil disturbances since he has been in office I think is eloquent testimony to his work."

In Spartanburg (Cherokee and Union counties also were his responsibility), Hatcher developed programs designed to improve opportunities and lifestyles for poor people. His most significant contribution, he said, was the expansion of the Head Start program for pre-school children of low-income families from a 10-week summer program to a nine-month operation coinciding with the standard school year. This involved restaffing several previously segregated elementary schools in the three counties.

"It was a complicated thing," Hatcher said. "We had to find buildings, new teachers, everything involved in starting new classes. We got permission to reopen some formerly all-black schools."

Hatcher arrived in Spartanburg as public schools were being integrated. The racial climate, he said, "compared favorably with that in Indiana. People weren't as belligerent about their differences of opinion. My feeling was the people here were willing to be agreeable instead of disagreeable. We went out of our way to minimize the emotional side and any strong outspoken opposition."

Friends who remember visiting Hatcher in his office in PCA headquarters in the Schuyler office building on Church Street said his routine there seldom changed. At noon, he stopped to enjoy lunch—a sandwich and a banana taken from a paper bag in his desk drawer.

Oliver worked directly with Hatcher during his years at PCA. "He came to us with a lot of knowledge about the poor and unemployed and how to get things done in the community," she said. "He got right in there and worked with the staff and the work crew. He was a hands-on kind of person. He liked to be out in the community seeing how things worked and how they got done."

After almost three years on the job, and with his garden beckoning, Hatcher began moving toward retirement. He left PCA in March 1972 and said the timing was proper.

"I was weak in human relations," he said. "I was inclined to think that getting something tangible accomplished was more important than getting along with people who had the last word on the matter."

In the early spring of 1972, Hatcher began devoting virtually all his energies to his garden, then in its developing stage. Now, there were many hours—dawn to dark—to plant, fertilize, grow and weed. The garden became his full-time mission.

Chapter 4

Winter

In the hard cold of winter, birds rule at Hatcher Garden and Woodland Preserve.

For regal cardinals, it's the perfect home. They cruise the edges of the woods and perch in the trees, their red coats shining against the spare winter background. Noisy blue jays bark at each other. Reddish purple finches hop about in the underbrush. A tufted titmouse, lover of the deciduous forest, bounces from limb to limb in a small oak.

Overhead, a red-shouldered hawk soars over the tree-tops, looking for lunch. The rat-tat-tat of a woodpecker can be heard deep in the woods.

Although winter is the garden's quiet season, there is color to be found. Huge camellia bushes show big red and pink blooms. The cinnamon-colored bark of the Natchez crape myrtle, one of the garden's most striking residents, stands out in the winter landscape. Hardy pansies give dots of color to the entranceway.

Visible, too, is nature's sometimes hard impact on the garden. Tall pine trees, felled by wind and ice, rest on the garden floor. Fallen oak limbs sit in fern beds. Branches have been sheared from small magnolias.

On January 2, 1999, a rare ice storm blanketed Spartanburg, resulting in power outages across the county. Ice coated the trees in the garden, toppling a few. The next morning, a Sunday, Harold Hatcher was out in the cold among his bushes, without gloves, using a small pruning tool to trim sagging branches, thus limiting the ice damage.

Walter Soderberg remembers another long-gone January. Wandering into the garden on a freezing morning, he saw a startling sight—Hatcher standing on the icy surface of one of the garden's ponds, wielding a chain saw, attempting to cut a tree that had fallen. "Just as I got there, the log fell through the ice, and Harold went with it," Soderberg remembers. "He still had the chain saw in his hands, out there in probably 10 feet of freezing water. My brother and I got him out of there. You never knew what he was going to do. I've compared him to Daniel Boone. I think he has some of those traits."

Now, after another winter storm, Hatcher has lost a few of his garden inhabitants. But there will be renewal.

Spring is coming.

🌿 🌿 🌿 🌿

John Nevison, a retired chemical engineer, moved to Spartanburg from northwestern New Jersey in the summer of 1976. He saw a Men's Garden Club exhibit at the Piedmont Interstate Fair in the fall of that year, attended a club meeting and met Harold Hatcher. They became friends and were co-laborers in the garden for the next two decades. Nevison was a key member in the network of Men's Garden Club volunteers who were instrumental in the garden's growth.

"He had a lot of fun working in there with Harold," said Dorothy Nevison, John's widow. She and Josephine Hatcher met in another setting and also built a strong friendship. "John gardened from the time he was able to scratch one out of the dirt. He had a great love of trees, white birch especially, and hated to see them cut. The garden was the perfect place for him."

Trees planted by Nevison—a 75-foot cedar is the most impressive—dot the couple's eastside Spartanburg property.

Nevison worked at Hatcher Garden two or three days a week, leaving home early in the morning to be in the garden soon after daylight. He and his blue pickup truck ran numerous garden-related errands, both in town and around the state.

Nevison died in March 1997 at the age of 83. Discussing memorials, his family decided that his remains should become a permanent part of the garden he had loved so much. On Easter Sunday, Dorothy Nevison and other family members spread his ashes under the limbs of the huge pecan tree in the garden. It had not been a request of her husband's, "but it's the kind of thing he would love," Dorothy said.

John Nevison's name became a permanent part of the garden in the summer of 1999 with the completion of the John Nevison Learning Amphitheater. Three walls of stacked stone provide seating around a stone stage in a pleasant hillside setting across the pond from the observation deck.

Many others, old and young, expert and amateur, would work the garden paths over the years.

If the garden awarded degrees, Patrick Suber probably would be its most successful graduate. Now an assistant principal at E.P. Todd Elementary School in Spartanburg and pastor of a nearby Baptist church, Suber was 15 years old when he first crossed paths with Harold Hatcher. Fourteen years later, he credits Hatcher with spurring profound change in his life.

In the summer of 1984, Hatcher hired Suber, then in junior high school, to work part-time in the garden. The pay was $3.35 per hour for 20 hours a week. It was pure gold for a poor kid from one of Spartanburg's public housing projects.

Suber had been dealt a bad hand. His mother had died five years earlier, and he and five siblings were struggling in a less-than-pleasant home environment. There was little reason to believe that Suber would rise above his circumstances until the day Hatcher came to his home for what turned out to be a job interview.

Suber walked the mile from his home to the garden five days a week. Hatcher posted his work tasks on a board. He mowed grass. He weeded flower beds. He moved trees from one spot to another.

And he learned about the straight and narrow.

"He completely changed my way of thinking," Suber said. "I had to fend a lot for myself early on. I had some big dreams, but I didn't know how to get there. He was able to give me a foundation."

The Hatcher speech was much the same each time, Suber remembers: Work hard. Save your money. Stay off the street. Stay in church. Hatcher took him to the bank to open a savings account and urged him to put most of his earnings in it. He helped him obtain a library card. He drove him home from study sessions.

"At first I didn't want to listen," Suber said. "If I had money, I wanted to spend it. But he changed my way of thinking in terms of education and finance. It was the first time I had encountered anything positive—and something that continued to be positive. He didn't take away any of the obstacles I had, but he gave me the encouragement."

Suber later worked part-time at a local grocery store,

added significantly to that savings account, was graduated from Spartanburg High School and went on to college. Now, as an educator and minister, he passes along lessons learned in the garden to teenagers of another generation.

The Hatchers lived in the house at 124 Briarwood Road until late in 1996. Josephine continued to teach at Spartanburg Methodist College and was very involved in community service activities until she was 75, and she continued to work in the garden until she was 81. Then, slowed by arthritis and bothered by serious headaches, she had trouble sleeping and developed other health problems. When she was 90, the Hatchers decided to move into Windsor House, an assisted-living facility near Hatcher Garden.

Long-time friends remember Josephine as an energetic, spirited partner in the development of the garden—and the community. Forward-thinking, innovative and described as a crusader, she was involved in numerous area organizations, worked tirelessly to improve early childhood education and put touches of her own on the garden blooming in her backyard.

"She was so strong," said Dorothy Nevison. "She did a lot of physical work in the garden. She worked right in there with Harold. It was their dream together."

Of particular interest to Josephine was development of a wildflower area in the garden—a spot for trilliums, Jack-in-the-pulpits and other plants often found in mountain coves.

Harold now lives in a bungalow, one of the houses he bought and renovated, on the garden property. He had triple-bypass heart surgery in 1985 and contracted tuberculosis in 1993. In 1995, he was diagnosed with Parkinson's disease, a progressive neurological disorder that often causes tremors, slowed movements and imbalance. Fortunately, Hatcher's health problems were diagnosed in their early stages, allowing him to redirect some of his energies toward involving others in the garden and its future.

Josephine's health worsened significantly in the summer of 1999, and she died July 18. Prior to her death, Hatcher had decided to restore the garden's wildflower area in her honor. The new section, which will be home to native flowers and plants, rhododendrons and azaleas, probably will be developed across the stream from the observation deck. "I wanted a section of the garden specifically in honor of her," Hatcher said. "We're looking forward to a suitable memorial."

Members of the family spread Josephine's ashes in the garden.

🌿 🌿 🌿 🌿

Those who come to the garden to work find Hatcher waiting for them. On a typical weekday morning, he is awake at 5 o'clock. He listens to the news on National Public Radio (the television in his living room is seldom on) while doing stretching exercises. About 6 a.m. he walks into the yard to pick up the day's *Wall Street Journal*. He prepares breakfast, then it's on to the garden for a morning of work.

Around noon, Hatcher eats lunch before returning to the garden, usually to work in the greenhouse or to take care of miscellaneous minor tasks. Now 92, he usually doesn't try to work in the garden all day. Before Josephine's death, Hatcher shared each of his meals with her at Windsor House.

In the evenings, he relaxes by reading, usually gardening books. He's in bed by 9 o'clock. He said he has always been careful not to waste time. In college, he put two loud ticking clocks on his desk to remind himself of its value.

Although stooped by osteoporosis and slowed by various other health problems, Hatcher continues to work six days a week in the garden, often surprising younger, stronger people with his persistence. In large part, the garden is a reason for being, and it sets the cadence of his life. Alice, his daughter, says he expects to die working among its trees and plants. "He still has pretty good muscle strength," she said. "I've seen him lift pretty heavy things just in the last couple of years."

Beyond the garden, Hatcher has very few interests. He has never hit a golf ball, doesn't watch sports on television, hasn't seen more than a handful of movies in the past 50 years, has no interest in fiction. He often doesn't sleep well, he said, because he's making a mental list of things to do the next day in the garden.

This begs the question: How did a man who spent 41 years—virtually his entire career—working in social-action causes and with the poor and disadvantaged wind up in retirement in near-total devotion to gardening? The natural flow of his life might seem to place him, even in retirement, in the kitchen of a rescue mission or walking the streets, helping the homeless.

"I don't have a real good explanation for that," he said. "Somewhere along the way, based on my experience of overcoming the misfortunes that lead to poverty, I grew inclined to think that too often it's a person's own fault. I resent seeing them almost deliberately fail and take the wrong road. I forgive and forget, but I think there should be a limit."

His daughter, Alice, sees gardening as the great therapy in his life, one otherwise filled with a sea of problem-solving. "I think he was genuinely tired of dealing with the personnel problems that accompany being the chief executive officer of an agency," she said. "He had really never been attracted to the one-on-one type help that is involved in such projects as teaching adults to read, and he wasn't fond enough of children to be a volunteer school tutor. I think he felt a huge gap between his values and interests and the people who needed help—drug-addicted men, single teenage mothers, homeless. He sees being in the woods as a healing and rejuvenating experience personally and believes it will have a similar effect on others."

Hatcher is the very definition of self-reliance and has been frustrated dealing with those who do not attempt to find their own way. He has given inspiration to many of the public-service workers who have toiled at the garden as part of "sentences"; but others have taken advantage of the experience to return to the garden at night and steal equipment.

Still, he plows on.

Without Hatcher's frugality, famous among his associates, the garden probably would not be a reality. He used his Social Security check and hard-earned rental income to fund the garden's early years while Josephine's paycheck was used to run the household. Since the garden's beginning, he has watched every penny, making a mental ledger of virtually every cent's destination. More often than not, his income winds up in mutual funds, an investment tool he discovered with some delight years ago. His savings now total an impressive amount, one he hopes will be used to benefit the garden long after his passing. To watch him pore over the mutual fund listings in the *Wall Street Journal* every morning is to understand the joys of compound interest. It is ironic, he admits, that he now benefits financially from the success of big corporations similar to ones he once railed against at the forefront of union movements.

He lives simply and is surprised that others don't. He doesn't drink alcohol or smoke. "He doesn't swear," said Alice, "and he doesn't listen to music since Beethoven." He has never owned a credit card ("Except one that Sears sent me that I didn't ask for"), has never used credit to buy a car (his Plymouth Reliant is a decade old) and seldom buys a soft drink. "Why spend 50 cents on a drink when you can take that money, put it in your mutual fund, and pretty soon it's 75 cents?" he asks. "I bet I haven't spent $10 on soft drinks in the last 50 years."

It's an attitude he developed early in life. He ran to the bank with the first money he earned in tobacco fields. Reaching adulthood in the Great Depression, he learned its lessons well. "From childhood, I remember him buying baked goods at the stores where they sold the old bread," Alice said. "He'd buy a whole bunch and stick it in the trunk of the car in the winter where it could stay frozen and last longer. But he also carried gasoline around in the trunk, and I remember refusing to eat that gasoline frozen bread. You'd open some of the cakes, and they'd be filled with dead ants that had eaten the filling.

"His clothes never fit. He gets them from the Salvation Army. He thinks a dollar is enough to spend for a shirt. We buy him clothes for Christmas and his birthday, and they hang in the closet because they're too good to wear outside to work."

His creature comforts are out the door, down the trail,

under the spread of a red maple. "This project has been the most satisfying thing in my life," he said. "The quiet relaxation, the health benefits, the mental and physical therapy. I've often wondered how such a simple experience could be so satisfying and rewarding. For a treat, I like to get a comfortable seat in a quiet part of the woods and stretch out and look up the straight trunks of the 75-foot poplars, sweetgums, pines and oaks. I remind myself that they are our oldest living survivors and that they purify and moderate the temperature of the air that keeps us alive."

Among his few luxuries: Rocky Road ice cream. He watches for sales at the Bi-Lo down the street.

Hatcher's reach has stretched far beyond his garden. He has participated in countless projects with other members of the Men's Garden Club. He was instrumental in starting the club's annual tree-selling program in 1979 and worked for years to keep the club's tree bank healthy. He has planted or assisted in planting thousands of trees along the streets and roads of Spartanburg—hundreds at one site alone, the intersection of Interstate 26 and Highway 29. His trees grow on Pine Street, Main Street, Church Street and Union Street, in city parks, on school grounds. "In some of those places, my fingerprints are on every tree," he said. Friends estimate that he is directly or indirectly responsible for more than 15,000 trees growing in Spartanburg County.

In his early years in Spartanburg, Hatcher worked with W.O. Ezell, another of the city's champions of landscape beautification, on several projects. "One of my great joys was to garden alongside W.O. Ezell along the downtown streets," Hatcher said. "He had serious health problems by then, but he stayed active. He passed on his garden tools to me."

The Hatchers were involved in starting the Spartanburg Science Center program, a particular interest of Josephine's since art and science were her specialties in kindergarten teaching.

Hatcher's work has resulted in numerous awards, none of which can be found mounted on the walls of his modest home. He has been honored by the Sertoma Club, the Kiwanis Club, the Spartanburg Board of Realtors and several other organizations.

The most difficult thing in Hatcher's long life may be the leaving. He wants the garden to be in good hands, a goal he realized more than a decade ago with the donation to the Spartanburg County Foundation. After work by an advisory committee and then a board of directors, the foundation hired an executive director for the garden September 1, 1998. Kelly Petoskey, who had worked for the South Carolina Botanical Garden in Clemson, arrived to work with Hatcher in the day-to-day operations of the garden and to begin detailed planning for its future. In October 1998, the board promoted Kelvin Fortenberry, who became the garden's first full-time employee in October 1997, to grounds supervisor. He has worked alongside Hatcher in many garden projects.

The board hopes to establish an endowment to operate the garden and then to make several major improvements, including the building of a visitor center and educational facility near the entrance. The master plan calls for the demolition of four foundation-owned houses (once renovated by Hatcher) along John B. White Boulevard so that the garden entrance can be enlarged and enhanced. Noted naturalist Rudy Mancke, a native of Spartanburg, visited the garden in November 1998 to lead several fundraising tours, and numerous other community events have been scheduled on the property.

Expansion is always on Hatcher's mind. He sees adjacent woods—he recently bought a cane to aid his exploration of nearby land—and envisions them being added to the garden. In the spring of 1999, Hatcher and friends were hard at work on new garden space, a quarter-acre strip near the observation deck. In May 1999, the garden property was expanded again with the purchase of land at 814 and 816 John B. White Boulevard, east of the main entrance. Formerly owned by Jimmy and Carol Deal, the property lengthens the garden's frontage on John B. White Boulevard and provides new possibilities for the future, particularly in the areas of street access and parking. A duplex on the property now houses the garden's first on-site office.

When the garden was donated to the foundation in 1987, the assessed value was $103,450. "What I paid for these woods wouldn't have bought a good used car," Hatcher said. "And that used car wouldn't have held up over three or four years. And the satisfaction you get from riding around in an old car is very different from the satisfaction you get seeing somebody come in here from Florida, New York or California, look me up and tell me what a thrill it's been to be here, that it's better than some big tourist attraction. When I first heard many years ago that it's more blessed to give than to receive, I thought that was a silly, asinine statement. Every year now, I see how true it is."

Those who receive what Hatcher has given over the years come for a long list of reasons. Some stroll through the garden on lunch breaks, taking a quick escape from the noises and pressures of work. Others come for picnics, their baskets and coolers and children filling the gazebo. Couples walk the paths hand in hand. A grandfather points toward a turtle leaving a pond, catching the interest of the two-year-old in tow. Visitors come from all over. A guest book near the garden entrance lists names from New York, North Carolina, Ohio, Florida, Tennessee, California, Illinois, Indiana, Texas, New Jersey, Pennsylvania, Delaware, Connecticut and several foreign countries.

Hatcher walks through his garden and remembers his grandfather Mitchell, a man who similarly walked the rolling acres of a farm in Kentucky a century ago. "Somebody said of him, that Mr. Mitchell never walked through one of his fields without leaving it better," he said. "That comes on down to my time. I can't walk through my garden without finding something that should be done to make it a little better.

"A sculptor sees a rock and can see what it will be when he finishes with it. That's the way I am when I see a woods. I see the big trees and the little trees and the way a path might curve through them and the different views that you might see."

On a pleasant spring day, Harold Hatcher stands on the garden observation deck and looks out over the creek that has no name. He wonders about the destination of its waters, for one day he plans to become as one with his garden. It will be a small ceremony, he said, there by the creek. Maybe someone will say a few words, and then his ashes will be spread across the good earth of his dream, living still.

Afterword

Kelly Petoskey

As with any form of creativity, a garden is a concrete manifestation of the gardener's personality, an intimate and personal window on his or her soul. Walk through the garden of any close friend, and you will find that even the most minute detail—the choice of plant material, the style of design, the spatial organization, the weediness and level of maintenance—all fit within the context of the creator. At Hatcher Garden and Woodland Preserve, the garden exemplifies the motto of Harold Hatcher himself: "Be different." It was a motto that Mr. Hatcher embraced early in life and never forgot, and no one who has ever met Mr. Hatcher or walked through his garden would challenge that he has been successful in living out that motto.

Mr. Hatcher's idea to create a public garden in his own backyard was not in and of itself different. There are, in fact, thousands of gardens and arboreta around the world that originated as private family estates. However, what separates Hatcher Garden and Woodland Preserve from other private estates turned public is the fact that Mr. Hatcher and his wife Josephine were not wealthy landowners. Humble people dedicated to a rich spiritual and intellectual life, they were unconcerned with material gain. Thus, when they embarked together upon the journey that led to Hatcher Garden and Woodland Preserve, they were limited in resources but not in creative vision. And when they chose to donate the garden to the community for perpetuity, what they gave was their life savings.

As unique as the man and his wife who engendered the idea of Hatcher Garden and Woodland Preserve is the story of how their idea came to fruition. Their vision was so strong that it attracted a community of supporters—volunteers and philanthropists—who helped to make Hatcher Garden and Woodland Preserve what it is today. It is a particularly remarkable story given its social context. At a time when cities worldwide are giving way to a creeping social malaise marked by a loss of community and sense of place, Hatcher Garden and Woodland Preserve united a group of people selflessly committed to improving their community. The garden now stands as a testament to the power of that partnership and to the integrity of the Hatchers' vision and of the community that gathered around them.

> —*Kelly Petoskey is executive director of the Hatcher Garden and Woodland Preserve.*

Sources

Brewer, Nadine, "Home to the Heart of Kentucky," National Geographic, April 1982

Dubin, Michael J., United States Congressional Elections, 1788-1997, McFarland and Company, Inc., Jefferson, N.C. and London

The Greenville (S.C.) News

Hatcher, Harold O., The Textile Primer, Social Action, Council for Social Action of the Congregational and Christian Churches of America, New York, N.Y., Vol. II, No. 8, April 15, 1936

Illinois Union Farmer, Farmers Educational and Cooperative Union of America, Illinois Division, Bloomington, Ill.

The Indianapolis (Ind.) Recorder

The Indianapolis (Ind.) Star

Kentucky Tobacco Facts Pamphlet, Kentucky Agricultural Statistics Service, Louisville, Ky.

The Louisville (Ky.) Courier-Journal

Mailloux, Jane, "Hatcher Horticulture Garden," South Carolina Wildlife, July-August 1997

Minutes, Second Regular Meeting, General Council of the Congregational and Christian Churches of the United States, Oberlin, Ohio, June 21-27, 1934

Minutes, Third Regular Meeting, General Council of the Congregational and Christian Churches of the United States, South Hadley, Mass., June 16-23, 1936

Minutes, Fourth Regular Meeting, General Council of the Congregational and Christian Churches of the United States, Beloit, Wisc., June 15-22, 1938

Mooney, Patrick H. and Majka, Theo J., Farmers' and Farm Workers' Movements: Social Protest in American Agriculture, Twayne Publishers, New York, N.Y., 1995

The Spartanburg (S.C.) Herald-Journal

van Willigen, John and Eastwood, Susan C., Tobacco Culture: Farming Kentucky's Burley Belt, University Press of Kentucky, Lexington, Ky., 1998

Welsh, Matthew, letter to Mary Frances Oliver, Jan. 10, 1969. Harold Hatcher papers. Spartanburg, S.C.

Colophon

The Seasons of Harold Hatcher moved through design as smoothly and subtly as a Piedmont spring turns into summer. This Hub City title is released in a first printing of 2500 soft-bound copies. The text and display typefaces are Caslon and Caslon Antique accented with Wood Type Ornaments. The book's designer imbibed less frequently during this production, but the occasional spirit of choice was crafted, once more, by the Sixteen Men of Tain. Their smooth, amber product, GLENMORANGIE®, proved both comfort and encouragement as the millennium deadline approached.